Victims of Webcam Hacking 101: What is Webcam Hacking?

CamiEyes, Inc.

www.CamiEyes.com

DEDICATION

Victims of Webcam Hackers

CONTENTS

ACKNOWLEDGMENTS
The Staff of CamiEyes, Inc.
www.CamiEyes.com

CHAPTER ONE
THE RISE OF WEBCAM HACKING

Human eyes are the windows to your souls. Computer eyes, the webcam, are the windows to your home. What can we see?

Webcam hacking is the activity of hacking into another person's webcam and activating it without the permission of that particular webcam owner. The remotely activated webcam can be used to watch the webcam owner or anything within the webcam's field of vision.

Webcam hacking is on the rise as malicious individuals and groupings spy on people's private lives; in a world where privacy is a greatly valued attribute, it is necessary to take precautions and prevent your webcam from being hacked. Whether inbuilt (as is the case with most laptops) or external, webcams are increasingly becoming the target of hackers as they try to outwit each other and claim superiority.

Webcams are an important tool for communicating with friends and family; they can also be productively used to carry out internet conferences and meetings in business organizations. They have made it easier for individuals to communicate more effectively and earn money. These important devices however are prone to hackers. Once a hacker gains access to a webcam, he or she not only obtains pictures but also gets hold of video and audio clips, further intruding into the victim's privacy. A group of hackers in China has recently established itself as one of the most formidable forces to contend with in the hacking world. They have successfully hacked approximately 1,295 webcams from 103 countries, thus gaining access into people's private lives without their consent.

In an even uglier incident, a school district in Pennsylvania is faced with a lawsuit after it was discovered that they were using the school-issued laptops to spy on students and their families in their private residences.

Thousands of computer owners have had their webcams hacked and the owner in most instances only came to know about it a little too late; this is especially true with external webcams as some of them do not have an indicator. An indicator on a webcam is an LED light that automatically lights up whenever the webcam is in an active state.

CHAPTER TWO
THE ORIGIN OF WEBCAM HACKING

The internet is a great tool in modern day life but it has been greatly misused by the malicious intent folks; namely, the hackers. Hacking itself can be a profession as some of the most notorious hackers have been hired by government agencies.

The main purpose of hacking a webcam is to gain visual access to the computer with the targeted IP address. The internet is the medium through which hackers carry out this immoral act. Through the input of long, vigorous and complex codes, hackers rely on the platform offered by the internet to find easy targets. The targets are deceived into clicking on viruses as they view pages and videos on the internet. These viruses are designed to embed themselves in the computer software and act as a bridge through which the hacker sends instructions to the targeted computer without the user's knowledge or consent. The computer, being a machine without judgmental capabilities, executes the commands. And the end result is a hacked webcam and a devastated computer owner.

Getting rid of these viruses responsible for hacking is a challenging task and an inexperienced individual would need the help of a software individual to get out of this mess. Contrary to the thoughts of some individuals, webcam hacking is not a walk in the park for a unskilled individual. The hacker is required to key in the right codes at the right time and execute the commands in a sequential manner. A single wrong move and the whole pack of cards comes tumbling down. Hackers, however have perfected their art and rarely lose their target. Theirs is an addiction and they serve it by hacking into thousands of webcams and are now spying on a multitude of people. One can only guess how deep the privacy of unknowing individuals has been intruded and the shame they have had to suffer.

As proof of their accomplishments, these hackers post most of the private footage on the internet; these videos easily go viral and the emotional damage inflicted on the victim of this despicable act only grows by the minute. It is devastating to the victim when the hacker invades the person's privacy; these victims become the subjects of worldwide embarrassment and this could lead to suicidal thoughts as a result of the invasion of privacy. Even with a lot of regulations and countermeasures, hackers are still managing to penetrate the internet and computer security stipulations and hack webcams at an alarming scale.

CHAPTER THREE
THE SUSPICIOUS ATTACHMENT

The attachment is the prime tool in webcam hacking; these attachments are found in an email or displayed on a web page. They are normally flickering to conceal the command directly underneath. From a permission perspective, the owner of the computer legally grants the hacker access to the webcam and even authorizes them to take a snap. Webcam hacking is not only about the taking of pictures and video clips; the microphone, being one with the webcam, can also be captured and this will mean that the hacker gets to overhear audio conversations. If the individuals happen to be conversing and exchanging sensitive information such as pin numbers and bank access codes, this pretty much exposes the individuals to additional fraudulent activity.

Attachments normally found in the inbox are known to contain harmful viruses. By clicking on these attachments, the viruses attaches to your computer and the end result will be a hacked webcam. At all costs, avoid interactions with such attachments and report them as spam.

CHAPTER FOUR
FIREWALL AND ANTIVIRUS SOFTWARE

As per the standards set, each computer should have firewall protection. The fircwall prevents unwanted traffic from gaining access to your computer and diverts it elsewhere. The firewall will only serve its purpose when turned on; all computer owners are thus advised to ensure that the firewall is turned on. This reduces the chances of your webcam being hacked as the hacker will be locked out and won't be able to send instructions to your computer and trick you into allowing the execution of the commands.

Installing an antivirus in a computer is a safe move towards protecting your computer and the information contained therein. The antivirus software has to be turned on, however updating it regularly ensures that it is up to date and that their viruses' definitions will be able to single out any new code that might be used by hackers to access your webcam. If the antivirus program is turned off or if it is an older version, your webcam has a higher chance of being hacked. The hackers will tap into it and intrude your privacy even without your knowledge. Except for the faint light signaling that the webcam has been turned on, there are no other visual indicators that your webcam has been hacked. Most people would normally fail to notice this faint light signal and the result of this has been thousands of unknowing victims falling into the webcam hacking pool.

CHAPTER FIVE
YOUR WIRELESS NETWORK

Quite a substantial proportion of the human population is opting for wireless network installation in their homes and places of work as a way to increase their income generating capacity. It is important to secure such connections and routers to ensure that hackers do not gain entry into your private space. This can be done through the use of passwords and modifying the settings to ensure that any unwarranted traffic is blocked off. Your webcam can be accessed through your unsecure wireless connection and the hacker will be at liberty to take pictures and record video and audio clips.

Some of the hackers have been known to have affiliates who work as technicians; sharing the same malicious intentions, these individuals work together and rig your webcam without your knowledge and consent. Once the technician rigs or embeds a certain hardware into the computer, the hacker on the other end uses a connection to gain access to your webcam and sends instructions. This is more so for external webcams which have a coding that is different from internal webcams.

The above discussed methods are commonly used by hackers to gain access to computer webcams and spy on the lives of the computer owners; be sure to countercheck the settings on your computer and avoid falling into the traps set by webcam hackers and their affiliates.

CHAPTER SIX
SAFEGUARD YOURSELF WITH CAMIEYES™

Webcams have been widely used to spy on the lives of celebrities; the information obtained from them, whether visual or audio, is used to blackmail the victim and compel him or her to give into the demands of the person behind orchestrating the webcam hack. It is however possible to block unwarranted surveillance through the webcam; this will enable you to enjoy your free time and space without having to worry as to whether your webcam has been hacked. Following the simple formalities discussed below will enable you to block the activities of webcam hackers.

Unplug your external webcam when you have finished using it. This is the safest way to ensure that your webcam is not hacked and that you are not under surveillance by hackers. Unplugging your external webcam means that the hacker cannot view your photos and video clips.

Covering your webcam with CamiEyes™, a fun webcam cover for you and the family. Whereas covering your webcam might seem like a drastic step, it goes a long way in ensuring that hackers do not intrude into your privacy. What's more, this is a simple task which only consumes a small fraction of your time; it will save you a lot of worry that would be embarrassing.

CHAPTER SEVEN
ONLINE CONVERSATIONS WITH STRANGERS

If you are serious about protecting your privacy and that of your family, be careful with IM conversations with people not directly known to you. Your family members and close friends should also be advised to avoid the same; this will greatly mitigate the chances of hackers posing as friends gaining access into your computer and hacking your webcam without your knowledge. These individuals will also use the information they access without your prior consent and might even use the same information to blackmail you.

CHAPTER EIGHT
CLICK JACK HACKING

Have you ever heard of the term click jacking? This is a term commonly used by hackers and it involves the placement of an access code underneath a hidden window. By clicking on this pop up window and without your knowledge, you grant the hacker access to your webcam. The hacker will then be able to download your photographs and even take some photos.

You as the user, by clicking on the hidden pop up window, grant the hacker behind the pop up window permission to use your webcam and microphone. This kind of modern day hacking does not require further permission from you and until the moment you notice that your webcam has been hacked and try to reverse the situation, the hacker viewed your private life every time you turned the webcam on for personal use. The faint LED light does little to alert most individuals that they are being spied on by third parties.

Everything around us is being automated; digital peeping is a favorite among hackers as it places them in a controlling position; watching their own reality shows and at the comfort of their beds. Click jacking makes their work pretty easy; by placing the command directive “Allow” underneath the pop up window, many individual mistakes this for a genuine window and do not hesitate to click it open. Well, it opens a channel for your life to be publicized by malicious hackers. At all costs, avoid clicking on these very captivating windows; most if not all of them come with irresistible false offers and before you know it, you are another victim of webcam hacking.

CHAPTER NINE
HACKERS AND THEIR DESIRE TO HACK

The third parties gaining access to your webcam do it for various reasons; among them are government agencies that are intent on venturing into the very annals of privacy for whatever perceivable reason. Others are just after making quick money from trying to blackmail the victims of webcam hacking.

It is important to look out for yourself and those around you and work towards ensuring that you don't fall victim to webcam hacking. By following the simple steps outlined above, you will be able to keep hackers at bay and your private life will remain your private life. If you think that you have been spied on, take measures immediately to ensure that such a predicament does not befall you again.

Hackers are just engaging in a game whose rules they have mastered; arm yourself with information as well and outdo them at their own game. Webcam hacking is becoming a popular trend on the internet today and it is extremely vital to safeguard yourself against these malicious hackers. There is a good reason as to why your house has a door, to ensure privacy. It's time to be proactive with avoiding webcam hacking and maintaining your privacy.

CAMIEYES™ WEBCAM COVERS

Patent Pending

NOW AVAILABLE ON

WWW.CAMIEYES.COM

CAMIEYES™ GIRL
CAMIEYES™ BOY
CAMIEYES™ CRITTER
CAMIEYES™ BOUQUET
CAMIEYES™ BUNDLE

"FUN WEBCAM COVERS FOR THE FAMILY"

WWW.CAMIEYES.COM

Made in the USA
Monee, IL
04 November 2026

67384261R00020